# IMAGES
## *of America*

# HYDE PARK
## ON THE HUDSON

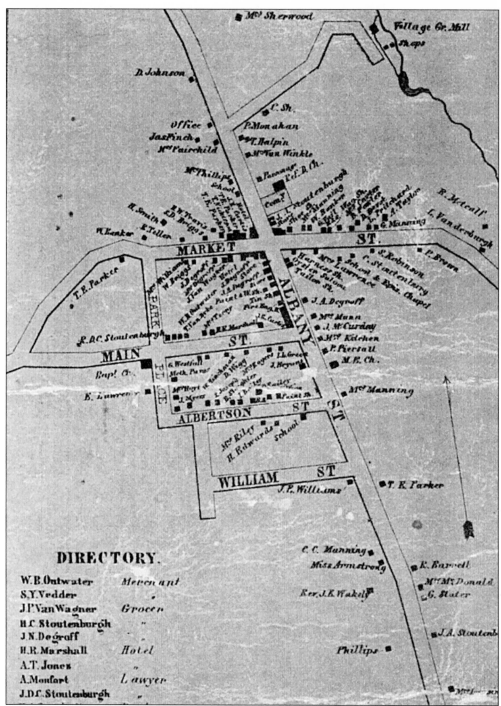

DIRECTORY.

| W.B.Outwater | Merchant |
| S.Y.Vedder | " |
| J.P.Van Wagner | Grocer |
| H.C.Stoutenburgh | " |
| J.N.Degraff | " |
| H.K.Marshall | Hotel |
| A.T.Jones | " |
| A.Monfort | Lawyer |
| J.D.C.Stoutenburgh | " |

*Map of the Village of Hyde Park, 1857.* Nothing is more interesting and reliable for the history of a small village or town than early maps. This one shows us the village center at the crossing of Albany Post Road (the King's Highway of Colonial times) and Market Street. In the map of 1791, Market Street is listed as the Road to Landing, the river harbor, and later the railroad station (which is still standing).

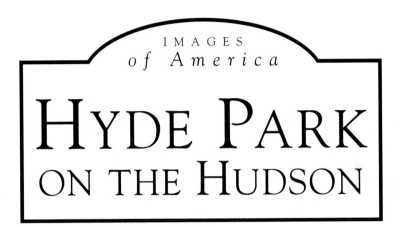

IMAGES
*of America*

# HYDE PARK
## ON THE HUDSON

Margaret Logan Marquez

ARCADIA

First published 1996
Copyright © Margaret Logan Marquez, 1996

ISBN 0-7524-0437-7

Published by Arcadia Publishing,
an imprint of the Chalford Publishing Corporation
One Washington Center, Dover, New Hampshire 03820
Printed in Great Britain

Library of Congress Cataloguing-in-Publication Data applied for

The Hyde Park Hotel (right)
Destroyed by fire March 14, 1879

# Contents

# Acknowledgments

Most of the photographs here reproduced, many for the first time, come from the extensive holdings on local history at the Franklin D. Roosevelt Library (National Archives), the Hyde Park Free Library, and the Town of Hyde Park Historical Society. Works by Charles S. Piersaull (1853–1921) are identified to call the attention of the community to this outstanding local photographer not sufficiently recognized. The section on Staatsburg has been provided by Edward (Ned) Leadbitter, together with the text narrated by him and compiled by students of Norrie Point Environmental Site (DCC) under Dr. Arthur H. Pritchard, site director. Pictures dealing with the fire department are courtesy of the company. In addition, the following individuals, representing their families or institutions, have contributed with one or more pictures: Mrs. W. Wilson, Bard College historian; Dominic Giambona (Anderson School); Dan Barton (*The Townsman*); Jim Spratt (Stoutenburgh-Teller Association); George Briggs; Bob Gilbert; Bucky Golden; and Kyle Van Wagner. The latter also let me peruse his most informative essay written while still in the fifth grade. Barbara Sweet entered the text into her computer and produced a diskette for the publisher, and her husband Herb helped with proofreading. Photographic services have been provided very diligently by On Location Studios Inc. of Poughkeepsie, NY.

To all and every one of you, thank you very much.

Margaret Logan Marquez
Hyde Park Town Historian

# Introduction

A community without knowledge of its history is like a person without memory. It moves around, but without a sense of direction. Yet historical knowledge, and far more historical consciousness, are not among our basic community services.

This modest pictorial history of Hyde Park is intended as a home remedy for that loss of memory, by providing the community with a graphic revival of our past. Some basic research has already been done by prominent local historians during the last one hundred years, and a few useful sketches have been published here and there from time to time. But a comprehensive, readable for all, old-fashioned if you wish, history manual of Hyde Park had yet to be written. All that remained was for someone to gather the information: we may lack other things, but not a rich past set in a magnificent environment.

Our present-day culture is definitely a culture of the image, and we are very fortunate in this respect too, having among our local predecessors some extraordinary photographers, such as Charles S. Piersaull (1853–1921), whose works (some of them anyhow) are perfectly preserved at the Presidential Library, thanks to the vision and dedication to local history of Franklin D. Roosevelt. Photographic sources are extremely difficult and costly to acquire and keep. Film is more fragile and volatile than paper and ink. The acidity and light cause old newspaper pictures to crumble or vanish in our hands, no matter how delicate the touch. Among so many concerns and perils, I have painstakingly selected these pictures from thousands. May they stimulate the appetite and will for better things to come.

Not only the specialist, but the common reader will find errors and omissions that should be corrected in future editions or in a work of a much larger span. There is a great deal to say in the short space available for every picture. And as for omissions, I am aware of most. Perhaps the largest and most disturbing is the silence about our history before 1742. A passing mention is made of 1705, the date of the Hyde Park Patent. But what about the explorations of 1609, so rich in description of our nature and aboriginal people? During my research I have come across some valuable references concerning local Native American encampments and excavations. But they need more than just a caption under a reproduction of an old drawing.

One of my top priorities in creating this book was raising the historical consciousness of the community. I believe that if we become aware of the value of our past, the chances are that we will preserve it. In this case, as in all others, I am counting on the cooperation and collaboration of members of the community, not only "old timers," who have been wonderful, but the young who necessarily will replace us, as spring replaces winter. Local history is about all oral history. Tell me your story, and I will tell you our history. You may choose making rather than telling history. That is fine with me, but better yet is President Roosevelt's blend, a maker and a teller of history, of local history, I mean, as he did.

*To my husband Tony,*
*who has given me constant encouragement and help.*

# One
# The River and
# Its Tributaries

*View of the Hudson River from Anderson School.* The tag designation "on the Hudson" is more than just a geographic marker to differentiate our town from others of the same name in and out of New York State. The Hudson has been the main historical factor in the development of our village and region. It is shown here as it probably was in its primeval state.

# 1609

# HYDE PARK

## DUTCHESS COUNTY

## NEW YORK

### Hudson-Champlain 350th

### Anniversary Celebration

## 1959

*The Hudson: from the Wilderness to the Sea.* This classic title of Lossing acquires a new dimension when referred to the historic year of 1609. Simultaneously and perhaps not by accident Henry Hudson, an English navigator at the service of the Dutch East India Co., and Samuel de Champlain, a French explorer, discovered the river and lake that bear their respective names.

*Old De Cantillon Store.* Richard De Cantillon, the son-in-law of Tobias Stoutenburgh, built mills and a store at the mouth of the Crum Elbow Creek, *c.* 1777. With a grant from New York State he also built the dock that became known as De Cantillon's Landing, from which he shipped corn in exchange for sugar and rum from the West Indies. (Piersaull photograph.)

*View of the River from the Southeast.* Esopus Island is in the center. The buildings in the foreground are those of the Sexton Estate named "Torham." The river is a mile wide at this point. Today year-round travel is possible, because a Coast Guard icebreaker keeps the channel open; there was a time when the river froze solid from shore to shore, making river traffic impossible. (Piersaull photograph.)

11

*River Side Hotel.* Old timers have identified some of the guests in the shade. From left to right are: William Curry, William Meyer, unknown, unknown, unknown, unknown, and George Bilyou (in shirt sleeves). For many years this building was the home of the Simpson family, who caught and sold shad during the spawning season. (Piersaull photograph.)

*Sexton's Boathouse on Bard's Rock, later Vanderbilt's, 1902.* What is known as the Vanderbilt's Boathouse was actually built by Samuel Sexton. It was the center of recreational activities and the mooring location for Vanderbilt's yacht *Warrior.* There is a tradition too about a ferry landing having been here "in the real old times." (Piersaull photograph.)

*Fishing Nets Drying Grounds, Hyde Park Landing.* Fish was essential in the diet of the early days, and the river had a good supply of it. Most fishing was done by net rather than hook and line. Between castings the nets were spread out to dry at the mouth of the Crum Elbow Creek. (Piersaull photograph.)

*Herring Scapping.* In the spring when shad and herring came up the river to spawn, John Bodenstein and Ralph Simmons tried their luck. While Ralph led the "stooler" (the first caught herring) over the scapping net, they hoped the herring would follow it and John would have a good hoist, before putting the net back below the surface of the water.

13

*Catching Sturgeon in the Hudson.* This mural by Olin Dows (1904–1981) can be seen at the Hyde Park Post Office. Sturgeons were huge fish that usually required help to handle. Pickling the eggs (known as caviar) was a business enterprise operated by William Meyer in the 1870s. The caviar was sent to New York City for the gourmets, while the meat was consumed by lower-income families.

*Clubbing Sturgeon.* After the sturgeon were hauled into the boat, they were taken to land and clubbed to death. Some were cut into filets and sent to Albany or New York where they sold for about 10¢ a pound and were known as "Albany Beef." Much was simmered and the oil sold to drugstores as a cure for ailments of man or beast. About 1914 the business was abandoned for lack of fish.

14

*The* Clearwater. Most Hudson River sloops were seagoing vessels redesigned to handle the Hudson's tricky currents. There were 450 sloops registered for trade in 1860. Some went as far as China. The *Clearwater* is a composite replica used for ecological awareness concerning the Hudson River. It is operated by the Hudson River Sloop Restoration, Inc., founded by folk singer Pete Seeger.

**THE CLEARWATER**

**The Hudson River**

**Sloop Restoration, Inc.**

*River Scene, Webendorfer's Boathouse.* Up to the middle of the nineteenth century the river was the main means of travel and carrying freight. Here we see the railroad advancing toward the north parallel to the river at one side and the Post Road on the other. The latter was built, beginning in 1703, by widening existing Indian trails. All follow the river. (Piersaull photograph.)

*Rider's Mill.* Located at Linden Lane, this mill was first owned by Rider, and later by Louis Traudt, who ground a fine quality rye flour, apples for cider, and feed for the wealthy estates in the neighborhood. At one time it was known as the Albertson Edge Tool Factory. It has a long history of owners. (Piersaull photograph.)

*Dickinson Mill.* The oldest mill on the Crum Elbow Creek, it was built by Dr. Bard as a grist, saw, and fulling mill. After several owners, it was sold in 1880 to Smith Dickinson, who operated it as a gristmill for seventeen years. His son Grant and grandson Sterling continued to operate it for more than half a century. (Piersaull photograph.)

*Carter's Dam.* The eleventh dam on the Crum Elbow was built by Israel Carter in 1866. He operated an edge tool factory there until his death in 1900. Carter was a well-known artisan and his products still show up occasionally.

*Cudner's Sawmill.* In 1850 Philip and Harra Cudner bought land with a dam and the right to build another dam, which they did. Harra and his three sons operated a sawmill known for its ship timbers, using the last of the original forests for material. The sawdust was used for packing river ice. The building and dam were demolished in 1926. (Piersaull photograph.)

Mary Powell, *Queen of the Hudson*. Launched in 1861, she was the fastest and smoothest boat on the river and made a daily round trip from Rondout Point in Kingston to New York City. The *Mary Powell* was a family boat: no liquor was served and there were no Sunday trips. She was so punctual that it is said West Point formations were timed by her bell. She was dismantled in 1923.

*Samuel Sexton's Yacht*. Most of the literature on the river yachts has centered around "ice yachting," to which some space is given in the section on sports. But the competition of family yachts, the equivalent of our luxury cars, although more subdued, was as fierce as the races on the ice.

# *Two*
# Inland:
# Clearing and Farming

*Rymph Barn, about 1768.* This venerable structure, the oldest in this collection, stands alone in this powerful Piersaull photograph as the symbol of an era totally gone. Almost all farmland, including that of the large estates, is now under residential or business development. The Rymphs' farm is in River Lot No. 5 on the patent map on the following page.

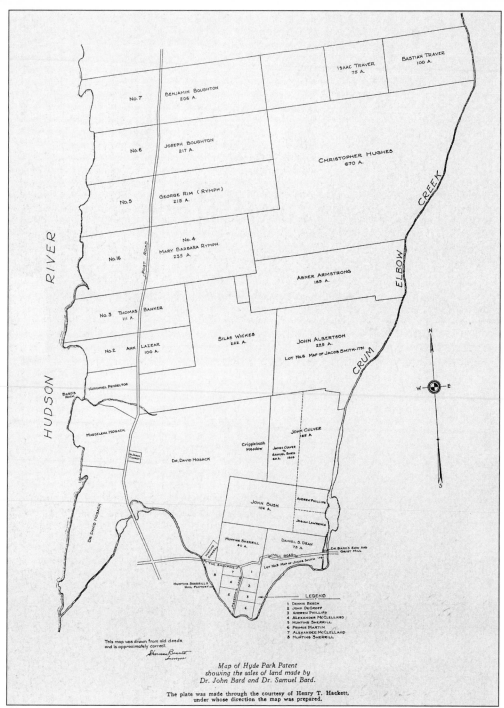

*Map of Hyde Park Patent. In Colonial times, a patent was a royal document to convey or grant public lands to private ownership. The Hyde Patent was issued in 1704 by Edward Hyde, Governor of the "Province of New York," to a group of men led by his secretary, Peter Fauconnier, who later bought the shares of his partners. Dr. Bard came to own the land through purchase and marriage to one of Peter Fauconnier's descendants.*

*Rymph Farm, Erected c. 1768.* Except for the Stoutenburghs, the members of the Rymph family have been landowners the longest in Hyde Park. In 1769 George Rymph bought land from Dr. Bard on the west side of the King's Highway and later added to it. He was a tool maker as well as a farmer, who had slaves for help. (Piersaull photograph.)

*Sam Mathews on Horse-drawn Cultivator.* Sam Mathews worked his farm the old-fashioned way, using a team of horses to pull the cultivator. But he was also interested in current affairs—he served on the first school board for the Central School District and remained on it for many years. He died in 1958.

*Clara Van Vliet on a Hay Rake*. Members of farm families all had to help. Here is Clara Van Vliet on a hay rake with a one-horse hitch, farming just like any man from sunrise to sunset.

*Alvah Baker*. "Farmer" is one of the most frequent denominations that we find in early censuses concerning the professions or occupations of those enumerated for taxation. Oxen were not usual in this part of the country, but Alvah Baker and his dog are drawing a load of hay from the fields to the barn unconcerned about their singularity.

*Walt Gilbert's Farm.* The Gilbert farm is not one of the oldest, but it was always one of the neatest and was among the latest to yield to development. The Gilberts raised cows and boys, and from father to sons they were baseball players.

*Mr. Gilbert and His Milk Truck.* Up-to-date milk delivery! Walt Gilbert is shown here with four of his six boys, ready to start his milk route. The method was to dip from a milk can to pitcher or other container and not to worry about germs. The pictures come from the family album. Too bad there is not space for more; they are as instructive as they are charming.

*Logging with Steam Tractor.* Technology was advancing! A steam-driven tractor is shown here hauling logs from a forest clearing; in earlier times this was done using horse or oxen and chains. Olin Dows's mural in the Hyde Park Post Office shows a similar scene; "Before 1741. Jacobus Stoutenburgh, his sons and slaves clear the land."

*Gilbert Farm.* It looks like the Gilbert kids are learning about thrashing. Usually, thrashers would travel from farm to farm with their equipment, with the housewife supplying a good hearty meal or two. After the grain was thrashed, kernels were bagged for winter storage and the straw used for bedding.

*Briggs Farm.* As on other farms, thrashing on the Briggs farm on Cream Street was an annual chore. The better the crop was the more the work, but the greater the savings for winter, too. For other details on this extraordinary family of Quaker farmers see pp. 70 and 77.

*Winter Landscape by J. Sterling Bird (1874–1944).* Together with Piersaull, Sterling Bird was an outstanding photographer of the land around Hyde Park and wherever else he went. Here he shows us the farmer and his companion dog carrying water and feed to the animals in the little shed. Winters were harsh, which made spring even more welcome.

*Roosevelt Farmhouse, c. 1908, the Author's Birthplace.* James Roosevelt's farm was a self-sufficient operation with horses, cows, pigs, chickens, a large vegetable garden, and an ice house to supply the dairy. Head farmers like my father (and grandfather before him) lived in the farmhouse, and boarded the hired men, who slept upstairs.

*Roosevelt Farm Barn.* The red barn was an imposing structure with an open wagon shed, machine room with watering trough outside, cow barn, and hay loft. In separate buildings were the corn crib, pig house, garage, dairy, and ice house, plus a pile of cut wood for heating and cooking.

*The Head Farmer and Wife at Roosevelt Farm.*
At the end of the 1800s and beginning of
the 1900s, James Edgar (the author's
maternal grandfather, born in Scotland) was
the head farmer, who managed the farm.
The farm was on the east side of the Albany
Post Road, while the mansion was on the
west side overlooking the river.

*Head Farmer Gilbert Logan, Wife, and Son,*
*c. 1911.* Gilbert Logan came to work for James
Edgar and, as so often happened, he married the
farmer's daughter, Jane. When Edgar retired,
Gilbert became the head farmer until his
premature death in 1923 at the age of forty-one.
Here he is shown holding his infant son, named
James, after his grandfather.

*The Rogers Farm Barns*. Rogers' red barns added to the rural atmosphere of Hyde Park. They housed a large herd of cows and several teams of horses. A bronze bell in the tower sounded the starting and stopping of work for the farmhands, serving at the same time as the timepiece for the surrounding area.

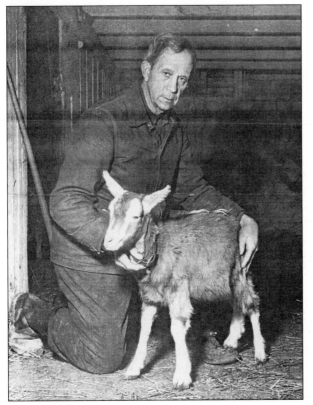

*Moses Walter Smith (1876–1959)*. "Mose Smith," as everyone called him, was a Spanish-American War veteran, who served in Cuba. He was the tenant farmer for President Roosevelt, besides being a close friend of him. Mose could not talk without cursing and spitting tobacco juice, but he was celebrated for his wisdom and loyalty.

*Vanderbilt Farm Barns.* These barns were designed by McKim, Mead and White, the same architectural firm who designed the mansion. The shingled exterior walls were fuel for the 1987 fire that destroyed the Summer Theater, to which the barns had been converted.

*Cows in Vanderbilt Barnyard.* Like all the area estates, the Vanderbilt farm was a working farm, despite its monumental appearance. It had huge Belgian draft horses, Jersey cows, white Leghorn chickens, and Berkshire pigs. The vegetable garden was extensive and the orchard produced enough to have apples for sale. Ice for refrigeration was cut from their own pond.

*Harvey Duke with Oxen Team.* In the early part of our century this team of oxen driven by Harvey Duke was active on the Vanderbilt farm. Imagine the smooth ride using a wagon with iron wheels on dirt roads!

*Chapel Corners Grange.* The national fraternal association for farmers called the Grange was very active in the southeastern part of Hyde Park. This group of people was the 1940 committee from Chapel Corners Grange, responsible for arranging an exhibit of their beliefs, history, and products at the Dutchess County Fair.

*Reforestation.* In 1928 the Cornell University Agricultural Experiment Station gathered data from the reforestation project that Colonel Archibald Rogers had started some twenty years previously. President Roosevelt also did extensive reforestation on his property and encouraged others to do likewise.

*Home and Family of J.K. Bahret, Violet Grower.* Violet growing in Hyde Park during the early part of this century could be called both farming and an industry at the same time. For information on this activity as an industry, see the map of violet growers and the greenhouses on p. 44. Note, too, the vintage of the car, 1920?

*Stonewalls Restoration Project.* "Despite last week's uncomfortable temperatures (a heat wave) Jerry Sadosky, Arlington teacher and Hyde Park Roosevelt High School student, Chuck Borg, were working to get the historic walls in shape." The restoration has been an ongoing project of the Hyde Park Visual Environment Committee for more than twenty years. (Text and photograph, *The Hyde Park Townsman*, July 20, 1983.)

*The Stoutenburgh Manor House.* This is all that remains of "this most historic home," a sign not inappropriately resembling a tombstone. The manor house was razed in 1870, believe it or not, just to straighten a small curve at the corner of W. Market Street and Park Place. Part of the grounds, 3.5 acres, has been preserved and is the property of the Gilnack family.

# *Three*
# Commerce and Industries

*Philip Rogers (1829–1902) in front of Briggs Store.* The first enterprise of the original settlers was a store on the landing. The small shops in this picture had behind them a long tradition of trading. Industry was artisan for the most part. The gentleman riding his gig represents big business families. They just lived here, but their businesses were somewhere else. (Piersaull photograph.)

*Briggs Store.* Hiram Briggs (1834–1909) clerked in this store for N. Vedder before spending much time clerking in New York City. He established his own business here in 1886, and became a prominent businessman because of his systematic and honorable methods in buying and selling, and his good selection of merchandise. (Piersaull photograph.)

*Hopkins Drug Store.* Located at the southwest corner of W. Market Street, this was the only drugstore from time immemorial. During all those years it went through many owners, with only minor changes in its architecture. Although the picture shows a continuous building, the Park Bakery and Joel Saloon were separate units attached. (Piersaull photograph.)

*Frank Hicks Grocery Store.* This site, on the northwest side of W. Market Street, was originally the location of the Hyde Park Hotel, which was destroyed by fire in 1879. In 1884, Charles S. Tilley built this store to be used for the sale of general merchandise, which is what it has been doing ever since. (Piersaull photograph.)

*Piersaull Fish Market.* There is very little known about Piersaull. *The Historian* refers to him as "Fishmonger." Here we can see his beloved negatives drying outdoors under the advertisement "FISH MARKET." In a dilapidated neighborhood in the heart of Hyde Park, the humble building and the glass negatives have miraculously survived. (Piersaull photograph.)

*South End of "The Row."* Route 9, formerly known as the King's Highway, and after the Revolution as Albany Post Road, opened the area to commercialization. Augustus T. Cowman (1814–1854), a gentleman of some wealth, developed the west side of the highway north of Main Street in the 1840s. It was known then as "Cowman's Row," and later, just as "The Row."

*North End of "The Row."* "The Row" was eventually bought by Jacob Zepf, and he operated a saloon and billiard parlor here. His son Albert later bought the entire property and opened a restaurant, ice cream parlor, and dance hall, plus several stores with apartments above.

*Fire at "The Row."* When the fire happened in 1967, all the buildings were consumed at once. Because the structures were so old, it was a hard fire to control under most adverse weather conditions. "The Row" held memories for the many people who depended on it for entertainment or employment.

*The Hull House and Cider Mill.* On the left below the curve of River Road going to the railroad station stood a handsome complex of buildings. When it burned down, the barn survived and was used at various points as a cider mill, dance hall, and a dormitory for men working on the railroad. (Piersaull photograph.)

*Horning House.* On the south side of W. Market Street was the Washington Hotel, until 1861, when George Fowler bought it and renamed it the Fowler House. When it was bought in 1884 by Michael H. Horning, the name was again changed, this time to Horning House. Halfway between New York and Albany, it was a changing place for horses. It was also noted for its good food and for being a place to hear the latest news.

*Wheelmen's Rest.* This was another place for travelers to stop and rest, and for drivers to get fresh horses. It was also the village meeting place for men. Later this building was moved on rollers, pulled by horses, up Linden Lane to be used as a private residence.

*Park Hotel.* Located on W. Market Street, it looked very much as it does now. Jacob Zepf originally owned it before his son Albert took over. The present building was built after the historic "Hyde Park Hotel Fire" in 1879. It was a hotel and a saloon before being the headquarters of the American Legion. Today it houses Gaffney's Pub. (Piersaull photograph.)

*Union Corners Hotel.* Big Sid McHoul operated the saloon in the Union Corners Hotel, which was built in 1820. When the state decided to straighten Violet Avenue, the hotel was in the way, so it was demolished.

*Daniel Wigg's Blacksmith Shop.* Judging from old maps, directories, and censuses, throughout the nineteenth century there were other blacksmith shops in town. But Daniel Wigg (see his formidable portrait by Piersaull on p. 70), whose shop was on the north side of Albertson Street, has come to represent all of them as a classic. He was one of the last and the greatest. Piersaull's father, Paul, was also a blacksmith and as such appears in the map of Hyde Park Village in 1857. (Piersaull photograph.)

# WIGG'S
# Whirlbone Horse Liniment

TRADE MARK.

Cures Lameness in the Whirlbone, Shoulder Sprain, or any kind of Lameness caused by accident to HORSES or CATTLE. Also good for Rheumatism, Neuralgia and all pains that flesh is heir to.

**Wigg's Horse Shoe Ointment** The Greatest Veterinary Remedy known. Guaranteed to cure Contracted Feet, Quarter Cracks, Corns, Thrush, Grease Heels, Speed Cracks, Nails in the Foot, Shoe Boils, Foot Rot, Harness Galls, Scratches and Mud Fever. Should be kept in every stable.

### MANUFACTURED BY
## C. BAYLES, HYDE PARK, N. Y.
### Wholesale and Retail by DOTY & HUMPHREY DRUG CO.

*Wigg's Whirlbone Horse Liniment.* Wigg's blacksmith shop was a prosperous business since he ministered mostly during the time of the big estates. But his liniment, advertised as being "good for man and beast" (no insult meant), surely earned him an extra buck. The fact that it was sold in the pharmacies of his time proves historically his point.

*Albany Post Road Milestone.* Some time before 1774, road markers were placed every mile along the Post Road indicating the miles from New York to Albany for the benefit of the mail carriers. While governor, Franklin D. Roosevelt asked to have these sandstone markers protected by fieldstone enclosures.

*Tilley House.* Here is the story of another early local entrepreneur. Was he the inventor of prefabricated homes? Around 1880, David Tilley decided to develop East Market Street, and consequently built three similar neighboring houses for $1,100 each. They were easily identified because of their similarity and as such were known as Tilley Houses.

*Hyde Park Railroad Station.* The railroad following the east side of the Hudson reached Hyde Park in 1850. Because of the estates, passengers were plentiful. Two tracks were laid at first, but they were increased to four in 1914, and then reduced again to two in 1950. The gentlemen gracing the picture are Mr. Farrell (left), the ticket agent for years, and Mr. Burger. (Piersaull photograph.)

*Twentieth Century Limited.* On March 13, 1912, the Twentieth Century Limited, the fastest train between New York and Chicago, went off the track at Rogers Point. Because the river was frozen, the cars rested on the ice as if they had been on land. There were no serious injuries.

*Cold Weather Work on the Railroad.* Putting the train back on the track required heavy equipment. Because of the cold weather the steam froze quickly, making a winter wonderland of the accident's site. It took two full days to get the famous train back on the track.

*The Telephone Office.* The telephone was a great invention, and by 1911 there were fifty-four subscribers in Hyde Park. This Parker Avenue house was the second location of the telephone office. There were many party lines, and the operator and neighbors could listen in on each others' conversations. Dial phones came to Hyde Park in 1948.

*Violet Growing.* Violet growers maintained greenhouses, work sheds with a furnace in the basement, and a tank house with a windmill for water supply. The men picked the violets, put them in water in the work shed, and, helped by women, made bunches of one hundred violets each. The bunches in wet tissue paper were wrapped in waxed paper and put in corrugated boxes for shipment. (Piersaull photograph.)

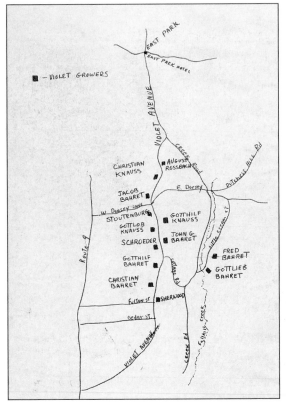

*Violet Growers' Map.* This map shows the number and close proximity of the growers. The operation became so big that the name Creek Road was changed to Violet Avenue, the name it still retains.

*Elmer Van Wagner's Buses.* Elmer's first bus was a Ford truck that had what they called "the Haywood Extension" added to it. After this, Elmer had yellow buses. There were about four runs a day, carrying students to Poughkeepsie High School, and people going to work. They also met the Day Liner Boat from New York to take passengers sightseeing. Van's Bus Line ran along Route 9G from 1916 to 1927.

*Elmer Van Wagner with His Bus.* The first buses were converted trucks: they had open sides with curtains, no inside lights, and wooden seats without cushions. They also had to be drained each night in the winter months, so they would not freeze. When they froze en route, Mr. Van Wagner would put his coat over the engine to thaw it. (This information is from Mrs. Van Wagner, who is lucid in her nineties.)

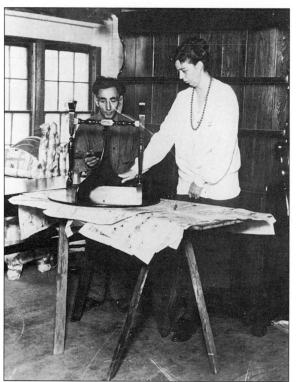

*Val-Kill Industries.* The enterprise was an experiment undertaken by Mrs. Eleanor Roosevelt, Nancy Cook, Marion Dickerman, and Caroline O'Day. The purpose was to give employment to seasonal workers. They made quality reproductions of Early American furniture, pewter, and woven material. Mrs. Roosevelt is shown here conferring with craftsman Frank Landolfo. The project lasted for about ten years and the products are collectors' items.

*Mrs. Eleanor Roosevelt's Home.* Mrs. Eleanor Roosevelt converted the furniture factory building into apartments for herself and her secretary, Malvina Thompson. After the White House, this was her permanent home, and it now belongs to the National Park Service. It is the only national monument honoring a First Lady.

# *Four*
# Estates
# and the Village

The *"White Bridge."* This graceful structure hides one of the first steel and concrete bridges built in the United States Crossing Crum Elbow Creek at the main entrance to the Vanderbilt Estate, it could serve as a symbol of the relationship between the village and the estates, strong though understated. Parallel forces, perhaps, acting in different but harmonious courses. (Piersaull photograph.)

*Bergh-Stoutenburgh House.* The oldest houses in the village, of which only two are standing, are what we may call Colonial Dutch: a one-and-a-half-story stone house with a gambrel roof. Mr. Bergh bought the lot in 1771, which his son inherited and sold with the house to Jacobus Stoutenburgh II in 1780—hence the designation of Bergh-Stoutenburgh House. (Piersaull photograph.)

*William Stoutenburgh House.* Jacobus Stoutenburgh gave his son William a farm on the Creek Road (Violet Avenue) just south of Union Corners (East Park). About 1750 a fieldstone house was erected, and it was enlarged in 1765. This was the typical house with a center hall and Dutch doors, rooms on both sides of the hall, and the kitchen in the basement. It has aged well.

*Odell House.* The second stone house south of the village on the Albany Post Road first belonged to Christian Berg. He gave it to his son-in-law, Martin Dop, who was imprisoned for being a Tory in 1776. His property was confiscated and sold in 1791 to the Stoutenburghs. In later years it belonged to Valentine Odell, who added the verandah. It was demolished in the 1970s. (Piersaull photograph.)

*Hiram Marshall House.* This was a family home, built in 1855 on land abutting the Washington Hotel on W. Market Street. It was originally owned by Mr. Marshall, who sold it in 1876. In 1886 Colonel Archibald Rogers bought it and made it into the "Hyde Park Social Club" for men of the village. After a few years, he presented it to the Town of Hyde Park.

*Old Post Office.* In 1872, this building contained John Green Briggs' meat market downstairs and living quarters for his family upstairs. In this photograph, one third of the space was for the post office, and the sign announced the Hyde Park Bicycle Club. Later, the post office moved to the other side, and it used two thirds of the building until 1941.

*New Post Office.* The present stone building was opened in 1941 and was dedicated by President Franklin D. Roosevelt. The building design was adapted from Dr. John Bard's house of 1772. The first post office was established in 1812, but not without some controversy about the name "Hyde Park" as the postal designation. The controversy, well illustrated by Olin Dows, has never been historically documented.

50

*Town Hall.* Colonel Archibald Rogers erected "Rogers Hall" to be used for the entertainment and benefit of the community. Since town meetings had been held in the homes of board members, the new building was soon used for town business. Thus it became the Town Hall. An additional room was added for the town clerk and later another for the assessor.

*Town Hall Fire.* On a frigid December 28, 1964, the Town Hall was destroyed by fire. The temperature was so low that water froze into icicles that hung from the hats of firemen, who worked all night. Valuable records were destroyed.

*Old Vanderbilt Bridge.* Two stone piers supported the wooden bridge over the Crum Elbow Creek as the Post Road ran past the Vanderbilt estate. Although traffic was not of great weight, safety was a concern.

*New Vanderbilt Bridge.* In 1898 Frederick Vanderbilt gave $18,000 to the Town of Hyde Park to rebuild the Post Road bridge. Being well built and several feet higher than the old one, it has survived the weather and increased traffic for almost a hundred years. The stone walls and stone buildings of the Dutch Colonial period had a clear influence in its design.

*Harrington House.* This Main Street house looks very much as it did in the mid-1880s. It was the home of Edward Harrington, superintendent of the Rogers' estate and later the first superintendent of the Vanderbilts' estate. It was often referred to as the "Domine Green House," he being a local Methodist preacher who also had lived here.

*Dr. David Hosack (1769–1835).* Dr. Hosack was a pupil and protégé of Dr. Bard. In 1796 he became an associate in Dr. Bard's office, while being professor of botany, his specialty, at Columbia College (later Columbia University). He is credited with the foundation of the first botanical garden in the United States connected to a medical school. In 1828 he bought Dr. Bard's estate from his son, William Bard, and turned it into a model of landscaping, most of which remains today.

*Dr. Samuel Bard (1742–1821).* The Bards are one of the earliest families of Hyde Park. It was John Bard, Samuel's father, who settled here first. His grandson, John, was the founder of Bard College. Dr. Bard is the author of important publications and the founder of the first medical school and public hospital in the United States, The College of Physicians & Surgeons of NY. He was also a great arborist, as can be seen in the extensive landscaping of his estate, which is known as Vanderbilt today.

*Dr. Bard's Biography.* The subtitle "the Man Who Saved Washington's Life" is not an exaggeration. Dr. Bard, assisted by his father (who was then seventy-three) operated on the first president of the U.S. on Wednesday, June 17, 1789, by removing "a very large and painful tumor on the protuberance of my thigh," in the words of Washington. It was an anthrax so malignant and so spread it could have cost him his life. He lived ten years after the operation.

# DOCTOR BARD

OF

# HYDE PARK

*The Famous Physician of Revolutionary Times, the Man Who Saved Washington's Life*

By John Brett Langstaff

ILLUSTRATED

Introduction by Nicholas Murray Butler

NEW YORK
*E. P. DUTTON & CO., INC.*
1942

*Walter Langdon's House.* In 1852 W. Langdon (*1823–1894*) bought out his family's share of property in Hyde Park formerly owned by his grandfather, John Jacob Astor. This included Dr. Hosack's estate. Although he spent little time there, he improved and enlarged the grounds. He donated memorial pipe organs to both St. James and the Reformed Dutch Church, both in memory of his wife.

*The Vanderbilt Mansion.* Frederick W. Vanderbilt made this estate his country home for forty-three years, from 1895 to 1938. Believing that he could enlarge the Langdon House, whose similarity with Vanderbilt's mansion has been overlooked, he found that the foundation was not strong enough for the house he was planning to build, so he demolished it and put in its place the present building, which was built between 1896 and 1898. Since 1940 it has been a National Historic Site.

*Vanderbilt Gardens.* The Italian Gardens, as they are commonly called, were built in terraces to the highest point of the hill. They were planned by James L. Greenleaf and executed under his direction. There were beds of annuals, perennials, and roses, and a fountain guarded by a statue popularly nicknamed "Barefoot Kate." The gardens have been restored and are maintained by local volunteers.

*The Pavilion.* Mr. and Mrs. Vanderbilt wanted to observe the construction of the mansion, so they had this building, called "The Pavilion," constructed in order to live in it. It was completed in sixty-six days. After the mansion was completed, this building became a guest house for males. When the Park Service took it over, it was a restaurant, and it is now the Visitors Center.

COL. A. ROGERS, MANSION,         HYDE PARK ON HUDSON, N.Y.

*Crumwold Hall.* Mr. and Mrs. Archibald Rogers completed their home in 1889, after acquiring five small estates to form it. Mr. Rogers planted tens of thousands of trees in his reforestation program, and was an ardent ice boater. They were known for their hospitality and generosity. It was a happy home for family, friends, and workers.

*Crumwold Stables.* Even after cars were plentiful, Mr. Rogers traveled his estate on horseback. The Rogers were good to their horses as well as to their children. They had a special barn for the hunt horses and another building for the hounds. The coachman lived above the stables. Their carriages were of the same quality as their horses and stables.

*Ann Rogers' Wedding, 1913.* It looks like May 16, 1913, was a warm happy day, when Ann Rogers was married to Griswold Webb in St. James Church. The reception was at the home of her parents, Colonel and Mrs. Archibald Rogers. Mr. Webb later became a state senator.

*Bellefield.* This simple and elegant house was built by the Crook family, who among other legacies left the Hyde Park a row of sycamore trees along the Albany Post Road. State Senator Thomas Newbold bought it from the Rogers in 1895 and left it to Mary Morgan, his daughter. Gerald Morgan Jr. inherited it from his mother and presented it to the National Park Service.

*"Placentia."* Located north of the village of Hyde Park on the Albany Post Road, this was the home of James Kirke Paulding (1778–1860) from 1846 till his death. A poet, playwright, and essayist, he is remembered for his association with Washington Irving on *Salmagundi.* He was secretary of the navy under President Van Buren from 1838 to 1841. Some of the material of his stories is drawn from the New York Dutch.

*Red House.* James Roosevelt Roosevelt was the son of James and Rebecca Howland Roosevelt, which made him a half brother of Franklin Roosevelt. He was always known as "Rosey." He inherited the house from his father. It adjoins "Springwood," and as the name implies, it was painted dark red and trimmed with black. It is no longer in the family, nor it is painted red.

*James Roosevelt (1828–1900).*
James was the father of President Roosevelt by his second wife, Sara Delano, whom he married in 1880. He was interested in breeding horses, railroads, and farming. He also took a great deal of interest in village life, serving as supervisor on the school board and the vestry of St. James Church.

*FDR with His Parents.* From early boyhood Franklin had his own pony and later, horses. Although older than most fathers of growing sons, James spent a great deal of his time with Franklin, teaching him about nature, farming, religion, and education. His mother taught him respect, kindness, and the graces of social life. (Piersaull photograph.)

*FDR's Home.* When James and Sara moved into "Springwood" it was a large wooden house with a tower at one end. They made alterations and additions to suit their needs and tastes. In 1915 Sara and Franklin, who was very much interested in architecture, redesigned the house, as it is today. Known as the Summer White House, it was visited by almost every high dignitary in the world.

*The Roosevelt Family Bible.* The Roosevelt family Bible, published in Amsterdam in 1686, had been used twice before by FDR when he was sworn in as governor of New York. At his first inauguration, as president, the Bible was opened at Paul's First Epistle to the Corinthians, 13th chapter, last verse: "And now abideth faith, hope, charity, these three; but the greatest of these is charity." This drawing was done by Olin Dows.

*Franklin Delano Roosevelt (1882–1945).* The thirty-second president of the United States enjoyed Hyde Park as his home from birth to death. He always came back to rest, relax, and vote, and was expecting to retire here to continue with his main interests: farming and local history. He was town historian from 1926 to 1931. This photograph was taken by the author on August 11, 1933.

*FDR's Funeral.* The train bearing his body from Washington stopped at the private siding and the casket was transferred to a caisson drawn by horses. There was the usual riderless horse with the boots turned backwards. He had selected a spot in the rose garden for his grave. It was a private funeral by invitation only.

*FDR's Interment.* Surrounded by family, diplomats, and the military, President Roosevelt was laid to rest in the historic family rose garden. He is the only president of the United States to have run for office four consecutive terms and won. Only death prevented him from completing his fourth term in office.

*FDR's Gravestone.* President Roosevelt designed his own gravestone and left definite instructions about what he wanted. It is "a plain white monument, no carving or decoration, length 8 feet; width 4 feet; height three feet. I hope that my dear wife will on death be buried there also and that the monument contain no device or inscription except for the following on the south side. Franklin Delano Roosevelt 1882-19—Anna Eleanor Roosevelt 1884-19—."

*Mrs. FDR (1884–1962).* There were many hats waiting for Mrs. Roosevelt to wear: wife of the president, roving ambassador, businesswoman, mother, grandmother, neighbor, and friend. She tried to attend to all her obligations. As chairman of the Human Rights Commission of the United Nations, she earned the title "First Lady of the World." She was. What an honor and example for us to follow!

*Val-Kill Cottage.* The little stone cottage completed in 1925 was built on land owned by Franklin D. Roosevelt. He and architect Henry Tombs designed the Dutch Colonial-style house to be used by Mrs. Roosevelt and her two friends, Nancy Cook and Marion Dickerman. The trio broke up in 1947 and it is now the Eleanor Roosevelt Center at Val-Kill, dedicated to perpetuate her thinking and ideals.

*Hyde Park, the Site of the United Nations?* This is the front cover of a well-printed pamphlet with supplemental information (there was a previous one with the Vanderbilt Mansion on the cover), presented to the UN and to the citizens of Hyde Park. "All but two families in the village signed the UNO petition," according to Mrs. Watson Golden. The petition was addressed to President Truman on January 2, 1946.

*The Khrushevs' Visit.* As in so many other fields, Mrs. Roosevelt was a pioneer of good Soviet-American relations. What is today common thinking and common sense, was then a curse. Just the same, she entertained the Russian First Family with simple refreshments at Val-Kill, after their visit to FDR's grave. Crowds were small. The village was used to this kind of ritual.

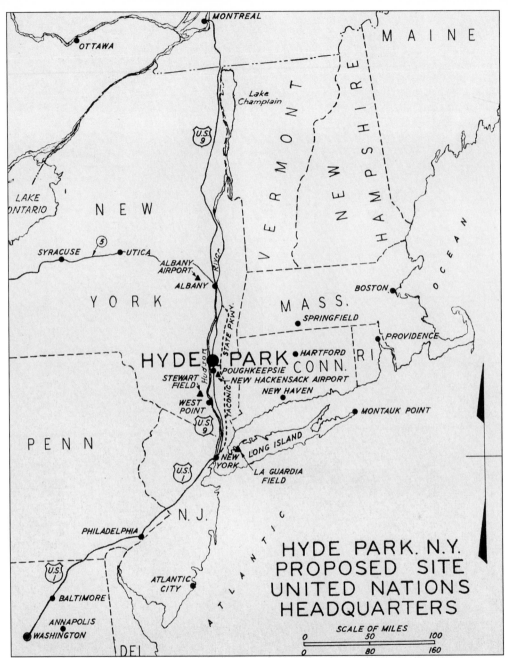

*The Map of the Logical Location*. With a photograph of FDR's home, the caption read: "possible permanent headquarters of the United Nations Organization. A UNO interim committee stated that the site must not be nearer than 25 miles nor farther than 80 miles from NYC thus making Hyde Park the logical location." A fitting end for "a village already known around the world." But it did not happen, God had other plans in mind for it.

*Five*

# We the People

*The Unknown Family.* The picture of this family all dressed up for the solemn ceremony of being photographed for posterity, is the exception of this community album. It came to us without identification. Fortunately, local history is mostly oral history, and the identification of pictures, an ongoing community project. Will someone tell us who this family is?

*The First Settlers.* These handsome photographs are reproductions of the portraits of Jacobus Stoutenburgh (1696–1772) and his wife, Margaret Teller (1696–1789), whom he married on May 25, 1717. The original oil paintings "on panel" were, until recently, treasured by their descendant, Mrs. Eugene Wells (née Mary Teller) of Rhinebeck, NY. They are now at the Museum of the City of New York. Some five years later the name of Jacobus appears in a deed of land acquisition, but the year of his final settlement in what is today called Hyde Park was 1742.

*Charles Sylvester Piersaull (1853–1921) and His Wife, Josephine Susan Aldrich (1856–1928).*
Charles Sylvester Piersaull, the first local photographer, is shown here in a magnificent self-portrait, as is his wife, Josephine Susan Aldrich. Little is known of the life of this great man. He is especially remembered by "old timers" as being a "jack of all trades," and was known for being very good to children, who he gladly allowed in his shop (a bicycle repair business), provided that they did not touch any tools. Piersaull is almost unknown, but not his work. In 1952, as part of the program of Community Day, there was an exhibit of his photographs with the evocative title "Down Memory Lane." Unfortunately, as Olin Dows once said, "Piersaull as a photographer had never been fully appreciated."

*Daniel Wigg, Blacksmith.* In the census of 1865, Mr. Wigg is listed as fifty-two years old, with a large family, and a son, Alonzo, aged twenty-eight, who was working with his father as a blacksmith. There are twelve other persons listed as blacksmiths; among them, Piersaull's father and his uncle George. We do not know the date of the portrait. (Piersaull photograph.)

*Briggs Family, about 1888.* From left to right are: (front row) David (in the carriage), George (with cat), and Alice; (middle row) Isabelle, John G., and Mary Briggs (a cousin); (back row) Mabel, Harry, and Theodore. There is an extensive, although uneven, publication of the family tree in America (1620–1940) by Harry T. and John G. Briggs (New York: Tyrrel, no date). (Piersaull photograph.)

*Tom Parker.* Thomas E. Parker (1816–1905) was a prosperous businessman and a well-known butcher. But most importantly, he knew it. His sitting for Piersaull's portrait reflects the characterization of one of his contemporaries as "Paulding's Butcher and Factotum." The last could be interpreted as "busybody" or a person employed to do all kinds of work. (*Paulding's Letters*, p. 429.)

*Albert Schryver's Daughters, Solid and Prolific Citizens.* Sometimes it was hard to tell to which specific family one belonged, because a large percentage of town citizens were descendants of these women, somehow. Descendants of two or three early large families are still very evident in Hyde Park. (Piersaull photograph.)

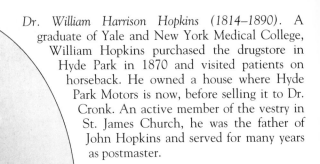

*Dr. William Harrison Hopkins (1814–1890).* A graduate of Yale and New York Medical College, William Hopkins purchased the drugstore in Hyde Park in 1870 and visited patients on horseback. He owned a house where Hyde Park Motors is now, before selling it to Dr. Cronk. An active member of the vestry in St. James Church, he was the father of John Hopkins and served for many years as postmaster.

*Sebastian Baumann (1823–1912).* The gardener for James Roosevelt, Sebastian is the grandfather of our centenarian, Helen Fink, to be 103 in May 1996. In addition to elaborate landscaping of the grounds, all large estates have extensive gardens and greenhouses to provide the mansion with fresh cut flowers and plants. Mr. Baumann was a resident at the estate, living in the Neo-Gothic gardener's cottage.

*Mrs. Kirkpatrick.* The Hyde Park Catholic population was without a church building until Mrs. Sylvia Livingston Drayton Kirkpatrick, a convert, built and furnished Regina Coeli as the finest Catholic church in the county. At her death in 1882, she left an annuity to help maintain the church and build a rectory.

*Dr. J. Sterling Bird (1836–1900).* A local doctor, Sterling's appearance was often compared to that of General Grant. Being public-minded, he bequeathed $7,000 to the town to build a public library. On August 1, 1947, the present library was purchased from the Roosevelt family for $4,500, using part of the "Sterling Bird Library Fund." His son of the same name, the photographer mentioned on p. 27, was instrumental in the donation.

*The Sleights.* Henry Sleight owned one of the early gas-driven cars, which was a great sensation. He was known as "Tink" Sleight, but despite his tinkering ability, he sometimes needed a team to pull his dead Oldsmobile up the hill.

*Fresh Air Children.* Every summer a group of city kids came to the country for a two-week vacation, which included fresh air, good food, fun, and love. A.T. Cook is shown here with a carload (you said it) of these children. Mr. Cook owned a seed-packing business.

*Mr. and Mrs. Albert Zepf.* These two were the talk of the town when they appeared in their fancy car, especially because she was the driver.

*Children on a Goat Cart.* No gas needed and there was no engine to worry about. Big brother John Watson Golden was giving his little sister Caroline (Van Wagner) a ride in the goat cart. Some goat! I hope it did not buck!

*Harra Cudner (b. 1824), Owner of Cudner's Mill.* Sometimes called Henry, this talented businessman and early industrialist ran a multiple operation at "the thirteenth dam" in the list of mills on the Crum Elbow. Assisted by his three sons, Henry, William H., and Augustus, they milled timbers that were used for building ships.

*John Hopkins (1845–1919).* The son of William Hopkins, John purchased the drugstore business from his father in 1893. His public activities were many, and included being treasurer of the school and fire districts. He served as postmaster from 1897 to 1916, under Presidents McKinley, Theodore Roosevelt, Taft, and Wilson.

*Ben Haviland (1866–1957).*
Benjamin W. Haviland, "Uncle Ben" to FDR, was seventy-six years old when this picture was taken in 1941, but he was warming his feet in front of his Stewart Oak stove after sawing wood outdoors. Like the President, with whom he had many interests in common, he was a local historian. He was also the author of a history of the Reformed Dutch Church in Hyde Park.

**Uncle Ben and the President Have History in Common**

Ben W. Haviland—"Uncle Ben" to FDR—warms his felt-booted feet in front of Stewart Oak stove in his farm house on land adjoining FDR's.

Mr. Haviland is 76 but when this picture was taken he had just come in from sawing wood—tough cherry wood. He first came in contact with FDR after World War I when the town asked Mr. Haviland to compile Hyde Park's war record. He says, "Mr. Roosevelt was kind of interested in that and took a notion in his head he would write a history of Hyde Park from way back. He used to come up here when he was getting this stuff up to find out what I knew." (FDR has written two volumes of Hyde Park history; Mr. Haviland has written a history of the Dutch Reformed Church in Hyde Park.) The Roosevelt and Haviland lines seemed to touch at many points. "Mr. Roosevelt and I got to talking about this," he recalls, "and he got to calling me 'Uncle Ben.'" (Uncle Ben called FDR's father "Uncle Jim.") He was a White House guest last year and went for a ride with the President. Of FDR he says: "A fine, genial democratic sort of fellow." Of FDR's mother: "More aristocratic." He says some folks refer to her not as "Mrs. James" or "Mrs. Sara" but as "Aunt Sally."

*Henry Hackett (1885–1951).* A bachelor all his life, Henry was a local historian, quiet, but very pleasant. He did mostly surrogate court work, having many "River Families" as clients, including the Roosevelts.

*Dr. James M. Cronk* (1867–1966). Dr. Cronk was a classic example of a family and country doctor. He retired from full practice in 1955, having served in Hyde Park for fifty-seven years. After making daytime house calls by bicycle (and night calls by horse and buggy), he finally bought a car in 1910. He was the town health officer and a member of the Fire Company, as well as being a member of several fraternal organizations.

*Dr. Locke*. William P. Locke was a tall and handsome young man when he came to practice medicine in Hyde Park early in the 1930s. He started in his home, but his practice grew rapidly, and he moved to a bigger office while constructing his own office building. He promoted the Northern Dutchess Hospital, and was a great chess player, but his first love was his sailboat. Sailing kept him going.

*The Rogers.* Mr. and Mrs. Archibald Rogers had plenty of property for their children to roam. Before dispersing to form their own homes and live their own lives they had a polo team. The grandchildren enjoyed the same freedom as their parents when they spent long summer vacations at Crumwold. It is difficult, perhaps unfair, to generalize about the rich families: each one was different.

*Florence Frost.* I am quite sure that if we were to ask Florence Frost what she would like most to be remembered for, she would not hesitate: "My family and friends, of course!" She taught her favorite class, first grade, for twenty-eight years, her pride being her two sons, Tom and Lou Frost, and her many grandchildren, with whom she is celebrating her ninetieth birthday in this photograph.

*Our Centenarian.* By the time this book is out, Helen Fink will be 103 and she will be reading it with a great deal of pleasure and without glasses. Helen is, and we hope she continues to be for many more years, one of the greatest sources for local history and the greatest of friends. She is also (don't tell anybody) the most dated girl in town. No kidding.

*Stoutenburgh-Teller Family Association, June 19, 1937.* The association meets yearly in the Reformed Dutch Church, the church of their ancestors. This family portrait was taken on the occasion of unveiling the Bronze Gates, given in memory of Roberta Louise De Groff Cantin. The first two families have branched into many other names and locations, but the roots remain here deep in the peace of God, by the river.

# Six

# Under God
# and Learning

*"Reformed Dutch Church. Rebuilt 1826."* Thus reads the medallion. The Foundation Charter states: "That the house shall be open to every well recommended Preacher of every Christian Society." In the earliest map of Hyde Park, from 1791, this church and the school appear together on lot No. 30. Separate by human law but together under God, the churches and schools are grouped together in this pictorial history, just as they once were in real life.

*Church Windows.* Dedicated to the founders of Hyde Park and the church, these memorial windows in the Reformed Dutch Church proclaim it to be the oldest religious institution in town, with uninterrupted services since 1789. Land for the erection of the temple was bequeathed by Luke Stoutenburgh. The lot for the adjoining cemetery was purchased in 1831.

*Crum Elbow Friends Meetinghouse.* Located on what is now called North Quaker Lane, it was built in 1797 and enlarged in 1810. The surrounding cemetery has been enlarged, but the meetinghouse, although well maintained, is used only occasionally. Early records were destroyed by fire at the clerk's home. In 1828 there were 204 members, all Hicksites.

*St. James Episcopal Church.* Members of the Episcopal Church in Hyde Park worshiped together with the Reformed Dutch Church until 1811, when, under the patronage of Dr. Samuel Bard, they built their own church. It was soon found to be unsafe, and in 1844 a new building replaced the old one. President Roosevelt attended it regularly when in town; and in 1939 he visited with guests: the King and Queen of England. (Piersaull photograph.)

*Morgan Lewis Tombstone.* There are many notable figures and families buried in St. James Cemetery. Among the tombs is this classic sarcophagus of General Morgan Lewis (1754–1844), an important leader of the Revolutionary War. In 1804 he was elected governor of New York, and during the War of 1812 he was made major general. He was one of the wardens of St. James for many years.

*Baptist Church.* The Baptist Society of Hyde Park was organized in 1844, and the church was built in 1846, with ministers in attendance until 1856. When services were not held, the building was used for prohibition meetings and the entertainment activities of other churches. In 1905, John S. Huyler bought the property and fitted it as a gymnasium. It is still standing as it was on the southwest corner of Main Street and Park Place. (Piersaull photograph.)

*First Methodist Church.* The Methodists began meeting in Hyde Park in 1829. Until their first building was completed on land given by J. Albertson (1834), they met at the school for $10 a year. In accordance with Methodist customs, there were many short-term ministers. In 1896 the old church was demolished and the present edifice built. (Piersaull photograph.)

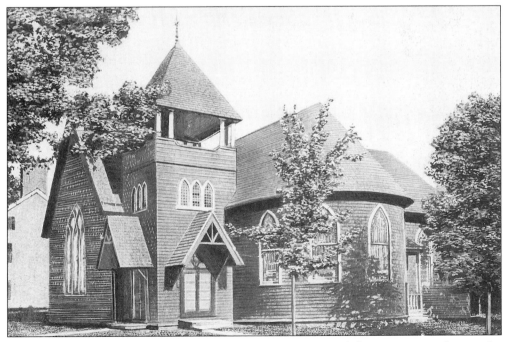

*Present Methodist Church.* By 1896 the old church was overcrowded, so it was torn down and a new church built on the site. The stained-glass windows were brought from Calvary Methodist Church in New York City by S.J. Huyler, a candy manufacturer with a home in Hyde Park.

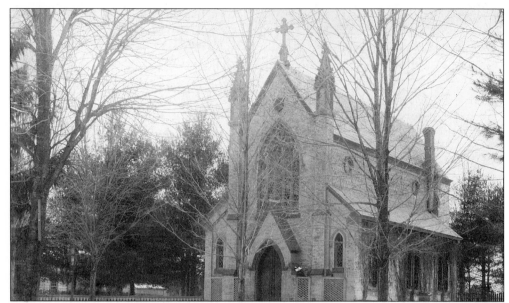

*Regina Coeli Roman Catholic Church.* In 1862 a Hyde Park mission was under the Rhinecliff parish. Mrs. Sylvia Livingston Drayton (later Kirkpatrick), a wealthy parishioner, built and furnished the church in Hyde Park, where she lived. It was the finest Catholic church in the county. This fine Neo-Gothic building was later demolished. (Piersaull photograph.)

*St. Andrew-on-the-Hudson.* Now occupied by the Culinary Institute of America, this large, handsome building was a Jesuit College for members of this religious order, known also as the Society of Jesus. The society purchased the Stuyvesant property in 1899 and the novitiate was moved here from Fredrick, MD, in 1903. The property was sold in 1970, except for the cemetery, which still remains in the order.

*Pierre Teilhard de Chardin, S.J., (1881–1955)*. Despite having been forbidden to publish his original essays in life, this important figure of science and spirituality died as a Jesuit Priest and as such is buried in the graveyard at St. Andrew. All his works have now been published in English and other languages. There are also several learned societies in the United States and Europe dedicated to the study and promotion of his ideas.

*Little Red School House.* The students and teacher (left) of the Union Corners School posed for a photograph about 1900. The building was built between 1845 and 1846, closed for reasons unknown in 1865, and reopened in 1866. It remained open until 1906, when it finally closed for good. Formally designated as School District #3, it has been relocated to the North Park School grounds, Route 9G, Hyde Park.

*Little Red School House, Interior.* In October 1972 Mr. and Mrs. Neal Condon, owners of the then disintegrating building, presented the schoolhouse to the town historian. Now it is maintained and operated by the Hyde Park Historical Society as a living educational museum. On a map of 1791, there are already two schoolhouses, according to tradition, one for the children of slaves, and the other for white children.

*Little Red School House, Class Picture.* From left to right are: (front row) Arlington Skinner, William Graham, Floyd Van Wagner, Ernest Wood, Loretta Pollard, Ethel Cudner, Inez Van Wagner, Carrie Burnett, Mary Welch, Clayton Van Wagner, Raymond Welch, John Peterson, Dennis Pollard, Paul Miller, Barlett Pollard, James Van Wagner, John Vail, Wilber Van Wagner, and Emory Taber; (back row) Almira Haviland, Hatty Taber, Florence Vail, Alida Van Wagner, Elsie Welch, Edith Burnett, Jennie Taber, Nellie Baker, Gilbert Schryver, Mary Pollard, Elizabeth Van Wagner, Blanche Cudner, Harold Rozell, Howard Lester, Sterling Dickinson, Henry Wicker, and Miss Blanch Adams (teacher).

*Hyde Park Village School.* Originally there were ten school districts with one-room schoolhouses in town. Some of them had been built by landowners and rented for this purpose. In 1829 a village school was built at the corner of the Albany Post Road and Albertson Street, and the old school moved across the highway to be used as a firehouse.

*Union Free School after Addition.* As the population increased so did the need for more school space. In 1869 a two-story brick addition was attached to the original building, and the village school became the Union Free School, with eight grades and two years of high school. The last two years of high school were completed in Poughkeepsie.

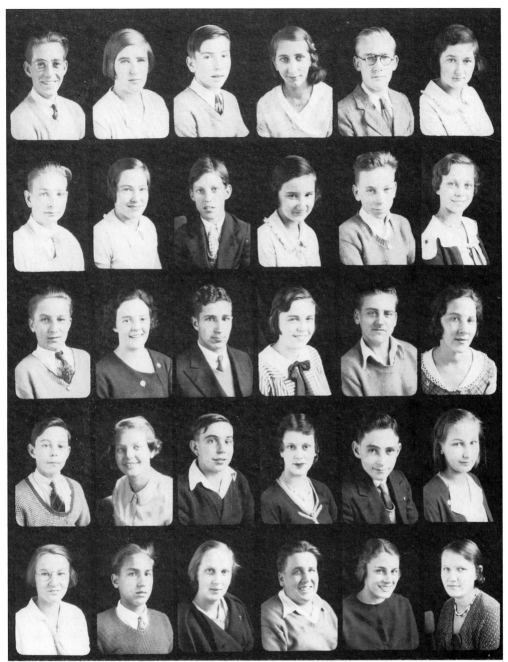

*Class Picture, Ninth Grade, 1933.* From left to right are: (top row) George Kipp, Frances Golden, William Leadbitter, Nedra Hover, Percy Horrocks, and Mary Logan; (second row) Harry Brower, Beatrice Brower, Fred Draiss, Jean Logan, Joe Sokol, and Victoria Osika; (third row) William Thorn, Marjorie Browne, Gault Applegarth, Doris O'Neil, Raymond Collins, and Lillian Kaelber; (fourth row) Carlton Kipp, Helen Matuk, Stephen Homiak, Louise Applegarth, Harold Kipp, and Marjorie Thorn; (bottom row) Katherine Werder, John Klima, Marjorie Martin, Archie Curnan, Virginia Ohm, and Frances Horn.

*Discussing Plans for Roosevelt High School, 1939.* In Ben Haviland's barnyard, President Roosevelt and the Hyde Park School Board discuss plans for the new school to be built. On the left corner is Mr. Haviland, who sold the land on which the school now stands. From left to right are: Ray Hill, Sam Matthews, F.E. Botsford, Arthur E.J. White, Alex Horton, President Roosevelt, Ralph Smith, and Thomas Qualters (bodyguard). This mural, created by Olin Dow, can be seen at the Hyde Park Post Office.

*Hyde Park Elementary School.* It was proposed in 1938 to apply for a federal grant through the Public Works Administration to help with the expense of a new building program. In order to get the grant, the system had to be centralized. This was accomplished, and work on the elementary school on Route 9 began. It was dedicated in 1940 with Orville Todd as the first principal.

*Violet Avenue School.* Located in the southeastern section of town, the Violet Avenue School was dedicated by President Roosevelt with the other two new schools in 1940. Miss Ethel Nelson was the principal. As the name implies, it was on Violet Avenue, very near the former violet-growing industry.

*First Roosevelt High School.* The very attractive Roosevelt High School, dedicated in 1940, tried to carry out President Roosevelt's words: "We must all strive always to maintain and advance our public schools as a bulwark of democracy." By 1965 this school became the Haviland Middle School and another Franklin Delano Roosevelt High School was built.

*Dr. V.V. Anderson (1878–1960) and his wife, Mrs. Margaret (Peggy) Anderson.* Dr. Anderson founded the school that bears his name, and his wife succeeded him as director of the school from 1960 to 1970. They are shown here at Mansewood, their residence. Dr. Anderson was a pioneer in the field of Special Education. Among his many publications are *Psychiatry in Education*, and *Psychiatry in Industry* (New York: Harper, 1929).

*Anderson School, Main Hall, the Administration Building.* The school's motto, "A tradition of caring for children with special needs (autism & SSEP)," is being gallantly continued today by the Anderson School Foundation, established in 1988 by Dominic Giambona, a local civic and business leader.

*St. James's Reading Room.* When the Bard Infant School was discontinued, St. James Chapel—as it is known today—became a free reading room, Sunday school, and guild room. It was here that the first public library was established, supported by the wealthy of Hyde Park.

*Hyde Park Free Library.* Founded in 1927 by Mrs. James Roosevelt, the president's mother, in memory of her husband, it was administered by her and later by the president as a family cultural philanthropy. After the death of President Roosevelt, the library was purchased at a nominal price by the town, using funds previously bequeathed by Dr. J. Sterling Bird.

*Mother and Son.* The close relationship between the president and his mother is well known. It is candidly underlined in this picture taken by the author with a $1 camera, when she was just sixteen years old. Her memory of "Old" Mrs. Roosevelt, who was referred to in her family as "the Madam," is of a kind and gentle, grand lady.

*FDR Library.* There were no two ways with the president when it came to architecture. All his buildings had to be constructed with local fieldstones following a pattern that could be called Dutch Colonial. The first Presidential Library has, among many other traces of FDR's personal preferences, a special section on local history, the president's life hobby and main avocation.

# Seven

# A Time to Play
# and a Time to Serve

*Armistice Day, November 11, 1918.* In this admirable picture serving and playing seem to be one and the same thing in the celebration of peace. This was a group of patriotic neighborhood kids identified by Bucky Golden, who is among them. From left to right are: (very front row) Vivian Golden and Nelson Milspaugh (in white); (middle row) Margaret Hedgecock, Margaret Freer, Bucky, Paulina Golden, and Catherine Hopkins; (back row) Hilda Hover, Vuelta Milspaugh (peeking), and Anna Keesler. The last child could not be identified.

*First Fire House.* The Eagle Engine Company used the former schoolhouse moved from across the street to house equipment in 1844. Unfortunately, the house and equipment were destroyed by arson. Note the striking similarity of architecture with the Old Methodist Church in Staatsburg, built in 1900 (p. 111).

*George Bilyou (1867–1933).* Young George looks proud to be a member of the Eagle Engine Company. He later became the village druggist, so he was near the firehouse, if needed. The uniform, not too far off from some of today, is what in the jargon of the young could now be called "cool." It was hot then.

*The Second Fire House.* Built in 1905, it was located on the Albany Post Road between W. Market and Main Street. The Eagle Engine Company and the Rescue Hook and Ladder Company each had a stall for their truck. The rooms upstairs were a pleasant place for the men to spend their leisure time. The two companies joined in 1961.

*President Roosevelt, a Twenty-five-year Member, 1934.* Although not able to fight fires, the president remained a member of the Eagle Engine Company. Shown here are, from left to right: (front row) Bert Wigg, Art De Groff, Elsworth Myers, President Roosevelt, Joe Plain, Al Zepf, Gus Hover, John Clay, and unknown; (second row) Chris Dolfinger, Charlie Moore, Irv Taylor, and Phil Andros; (third row) Bucky Golden, Robert Rose, Floyd Mason, and George Penny; (back row) Tubby Curnan, Harold Clay, and Big Bill Schryver.

*Rescue Fife, Drum and Bugle Corps, 1934.* Harry Kimlin was the leader, and Dr. J. Chatterton was the drum major. This was a really good corps, winning many awards not only for their playing, but also for their appearance. They had maroon jackets with gold-colored buttons and braid, white shirts, black ties, white trousers with maroon stripe, and maroon hats with gold trim.

*First Ambulance.* The first fire company ambulance was a 1952 Packard donated by Morris Cantor, car dealer. Shown here are Harold Farley, David Ray, Clayton Ray (driver), and Alfred Overfield. The Rescue Squad has been a great blessing to the community, caring for the sick, injured, accident victims, and the elderly.

*Park Lodge, No. 203, IOOF, 1900.* The Independent Order of Odd Fellows was active in Hyde Park for over a century. From left to right are: (front row) Robert C. Halpin and Fred Upright; (middle row) T.J. Herrick, Julius Pink, Edward Briggs, Charles Wicker, and Harvey Brower; (back row) John D. Wicker, T.J. Northrop, Henry Myers, H.F. Van De Water, James De Groff, Alfred Christmas, E.M. Taber, B.J. Burdick, and E.M. Crapser.

*J.K. Club.* We do not know what J.K. stood for (they were very secretive about the name), but we do know who these stylish ladies are. From left to right are: Mamie Traudt Rymph, Marjorie McCurdy Harden, Bessie Brooks Leadbitter, Nellie Moore, Beatrice Cummings, Mildred Bilyou, Mary Meagher, Fannie Briggs, and Elsie Christmas Townsend.

*Hyde Park Rebecca Lodge.* All dressed for a formal procedure, these ladies are, from left to right: (front row) Violet Rogers, Etta Robinson, and Grace Terpening; (back row) Betty Lane, Edith Nichols, Helen Nichols, Elsie Upright, and Gladys Brower.

*Boy Scouts at Camp Noteeming, 1948.* We can identify only a few of these boys. Do you know anyone else? Come forward and tell. Beginning on the far left in the front row, and moving from left to right, we can identify: (front row) Walter Browne (4); (middle row) Reed Myers (3), Mike Feder (4), Bobby Terpening (6), and Elmer Van Wagner (8); (back row) Dick Whitney (1), Peabody (3), John Brown (4), and Clifford Pitcher (7).

*Ellen Roosevelt (1868–1934).* In 1890 Ellen won the U.S. Singles Championship from Irish champion M.E. Cahill at the Philadelphia Cricket Club. After a very active life of sports, good education, and travel, she was happy to spend her time in the family home, living like a Victorian lady. She and her sister Grace were first cousins to President Roosevelt.

*Grace Roosevelt.* Grace was her sister's tennis partner; she thought their costume was "ridiculous." For tennis they wore felt sailor hats, high-collared jerseys, skirts with a 4-yard hem line (just clearing the court), and layers of unmentionables beneath. Grace married Appleton Clark and had a family.

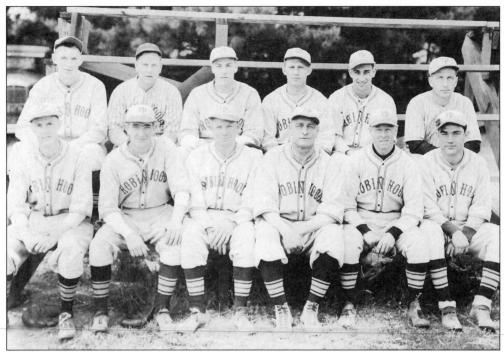

*The Robin Hoods.* In 1912 the first Robin Hood team was organized, and it went on to be an outstanding team for years and years. This team included, from left to right: (front row) Ira Browne, Gordon Plass, Fritz Kraayerbrink, Art De Groff, Bob Alquist, and Ray Schryver; (back row) unknown, Fritz Gilbert, Howard Velie, unknown, John Forbes, and Adrian Gilbert.

*Another Robin Hood Team.* With time the team changed. From left to right are: (front row) Bob Alquist, Ira Browne, ? Elwell, Lou Hover, Henry B. Schryver, and Art De Groff; (middle row) Jim Logan, Walt McKean, Ray Todd, Al Paul, Don Todd, and George Penny; (top row) Ted Losee, Fritz Kraayenbrink, Herm Plass, Jack Gilbert, Orville Todd, and Fred Sievers.

*Hyde Park Girls' Basketball Team, County Champions in 1931.* From left to right are: Hilda Hover, Alice McConnell, Margaret Oakley, Helen Dolfinger, Virginia Hedgecock, Helen Farley, Louise Coleman, Hazel Velie, Dorothy Oakley, Ruth Velie, Margaret Logan, and Sarah Logan.

*Hyde Park Boys' Basketball Team, 1931/32.* From left to right are: (seated) Carlton Kipp; (front row) Milton Rogers, Bud Wicker, Russell Schryver, Orville Todd, John Baril, Jimmy Stokes, and Nat Greene; (back row) Principal Walter McKean, Harold Kipp, Bucky Golden, Charles Welch, Archie Curnan, Al Tobias, Jack Gilbert, and Gordon Post.

*Ice Boating.* Ice boating was a very popular sport. As soon as the river froze solid, the fun began. When there was a good wind, the boaters would race the trains and could pass them. John Roosevelt's *Icicle* and Archie Rogers' *Jack Frost* were the champions. Not until after World War II did a Coast Guard ice breaker keep the river open for winter travel.

*The Regular Ice Boaters, 1959.* Art De Groff, Kunze Todd, and Tom Gilbert had their own ice boats and were always willing to share rides. Floyd Mason, Leslie Green, Tom Gilbert, Arnold Brower, Art De Groff, Kunze Todd, and Nairn Miller (in front) are shown here. For the author it was a cold ride, sometimes bumpy, and very scary.

*The Liberty Ball, 1917.* During World War I, to attract attendance for the sale of Liberty Bonds to help finance the war, a large ball was rolled by hand from Buffalo to New York. It was an unusual sight to see, so the townspeople turned out to witness it.

*Liberty Ball Procession.* The Hyde Park Boy Scouts met the ball in Staatsburg and escorted it to Poughkeepsie. It created plenty of excitement. There are, however, no records of the results.

*War Monuments.* There are three war monuments displayed on the lawn of the Town Hall in memory of those who fought in the four most recent major conflicts involving the United States: World War I, World War II and the Korean War, and Vietnam. On the World War II and Korean Conflict monument alone there are 503 names of Hyde Park citizens. Nineteen of them made the supreme sacrifice.

*Hyde Park Women Patriots of World War II.* The names of those who served are: Arlene Brooks, Wilma Clinton, Ruth E. Collins, Bertha Craft, Ave Marie Downes, Lenore Downes, Doris J. Golden, Alyda Kendall, Frances Kilma, Marjorie Lasher, Anna Logan (shown here), Elnora Merte, Mary H. Norton, Dorothea K. Scott, Angelina Sinbaldi, Lillian Van Ackooy, Mary Louise Van Wagner, Rose Van Wagner, and Evelyn Wigg.

*Eight*

# Staatsburg

*Stagecoach Stop.* There is little documentation concerning this charming old building. It is the first one we see, coming into Staatsburg from Hyde Park on the east side of the Old Post Road. Tradition has it that it was for many years a stagecoach stop, halfway between New York and Albany. Regardless, the building is emblematic of the romantic hamlet.

*Old Saint Margaret.* In 1858 this building served as a non-denominational chapel. In 1882 it became a parish of the Episcopal Church under the appellation of Saint Margaret. With the completion of the new church in 1898, this building became a reading room and, later, the hamlet's public library. (Piersaull photograph.)

*New Saint Margaret.* Built of stone quarried on Dr. Lee's property, the cornerstone was laid in 1891 and the church consecrated in 1898. The congregation was composed of "river families" as well as villagers. The building is particularly admired for its medieval windows imported from Europe, as gifts from Ogden Mills, whose mansion appears on p. 118.

*Methodist Church.* In 1876 the Bethel Methodist Episcopal Church was erected and donated to the hamlet by George Lamoree. This was a great convenience for those parishioners who did not have a car. But as cars became more common, this church, which was a mission of the Hyde Park Methodist Church, was no longer needed. It closed in 1969.

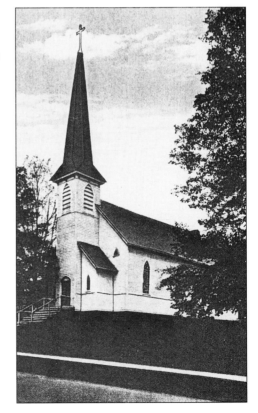

*Catholic Church.* Since its erection in 1887, St. Paul's Roman Catholic Church has served Staatsburg as a mission of Regina Coeli in Hyde Park. There are reliable accounts of a previous chapel located on Clay Hill. By 1860 there were seven Catholic churches in Dutchess County, and among them is listed Staatsburg's, which opened in 1851.

*Ice Cutting.* Ice cutting on the Hudson was a big winter industry, because it meant work for the seasonal workers on the estates. The best ice was early in the season. As soon as it was thick and clear, the cutting began, using horse-drawn and hand tools. The ice was marked into blocks and cut with saws.

*Working River Ice, 1890.* After the ice had been cut into blocks, it was moved along an open channel with spears. The pay was from 50¢ to $1 a day, with the supervisors receiving between $1.25 and $1.75 a day. It was a long cold day, and what could $1 buy in 1890? It would be most interesting to find out.

*Ice Conveyor to Ice House, 1900.* The ice was pushed to a motorized conveyor which carried it into the ice house. Once inside, it was covered with sawdust as insulation, so the blocks did not touch each other. In the summer it was again packed with sawdust to travel in company-owned barges to be sold in New York and Albany.

*Consolidated Ice Co. Storage House, 1900.* The ice storage houses, owned by commercial companies, were huge. They could contain up to 75,000 tons of ice. Most of the large estates had their own ponds and ice houses. This continued until electric refrigeration became common. Both the operation and the houses are a thing of the forgotten past, but what a past they had!

*Original Bodenstein Ice Tool Factory, 1920.* Because of the ice-cutting business, there was a need for proper tools to do a good and speedy job. In 1858 a German immigrant, John Henry Bodenstein, with a capital of $250, established a tool-manufacturing business at Staatsburg. The business grew rapidly and the tools were shipped around the country.

*Ice Tool Factory Fire.* Like so many other buildings made of wood, the factory burned just before World War I, but it was quickly rebuilt and continued to produce until 1984. In its latter years it completed orders for special products for the United States government.

*Ice Tool Factory Workers, before 1919.* Workers and bosses take a break to pose for this photograph, which will unite them together forever. Their products are collectors' items today; they were made to last and marked in a way that makes them easily identifiable.

*Exhibit of Ice Tools.* In the Piersaull Collection at the FDR Library in Hyde Park, there are quite a few excellent pictures dedicated to portraying the workers and their finely designed products. Piersaull is credited by Rocky Andros for having invented a gadget to sharpen at one time both sides of the ice boat runners.

*Blacksmith Shop.* The weathervane horse on the roof peak indicates the use of the building on River Road in 1888. The blacksmith shop appears to have been of interest to kids as well as a necessity for horse owners. The whole village must have heard the ring of the anvil.

*Kidder's Cedar Peg Factory.* At the beginning of the century, another flourishing business in Staatsburg was the Kidder's Factory, located on the west side of River Road. These pegs were tied in bundles and shipped along the east coast to be used in closing worm holes in boats.

*For Rent on Sundays.* A real entrepreneur, Al Schryver rented his car on Sunday afternoons for rides to Hudson (25 miles) for $1.50. Pictured here in the front seat are Mr. Schryver and Hilda Blair, with Dorothy Dodd, Alice Blair, and Mrs. Blair in the back. Style at its best!

*Hughes' Delivery Truck.* Ed Hughes rode in style in his delivery truck with Bart Hines as the driver. Ed's wife, Ada, greeted them never knowing what to expect, whether delivery or company for lunch.

*Morgan Lewis Home, 1832.* Morgan Lewis (1754–1844) was elected the third governor of New York State in 1804. During his administration, the final basis for a public school system of education was established. He was also one of the founders of New York University. This was his second home, the first one having burned in 1795.

*Mills Mansion.* A state museum today, it was built around Morgan Lewis's second house and contains some of his furnishings. Darius Mills, the father of Ogden Mills, purchased the estate from descendants of Morgan Lewis. Darius expanded and developed it using a fortune he reportedly received from enterprises connected with the 1849 Gold Rush.

*William B. Dinsmore (1810–1888).* In 1856 Mr. Dinsmore became president of Adams Express Co., which had affiliations with almost all the railroads in this country. Later, because of the Civil War, all the southern connections were sold to stockholders. He built his home in Staatsburg in 1871/72, and was generous to the community, giving land for the school, the firehouse, and the golf course.

*"The Locust."* The Dinsmore estate of that name had 1,000 acres of land and half a mile of river frontage. The house had ninety rooms, one of which was named "Gen. U.S. Grant" for the frequent visitor. There was a herd of two hundred Jersey cows and the stable held twenty farm and eighteen carriage horses. Being particularly interested in horticulture, Mr. Dinsmore maintained numerous greenhouses. The main building was demolished in 1941.

*Huntington's House—"Hopeland," 1909.* Robert Palmer Huntington (b. 1869) was, according to his official biographer, "A Democrat in politics and an Episcopalian in religion." A graduate from Phillips Exeter (NH) and Yale University, he married Helen G. Dinsmore in 1892. In 1908 he retired from the architectural firm of Hoppin, Koen & Huntington in order to reside in Staatsburg. "Hopeland" was demolished in the 1950s.

*The Hoyt House—"Point House."* Built under the supervision of Calvert Vaux, a partner of Andrew Jackson Downing, this house was a solid happy home. Unwillingly, Mrs. Hoyt had to abandon and surrender her home to the state under eminent domain law. The state did not maintain it, so it went to ruins.

*Lewis Gordon Norrie.* The idyll of this picture between a handsome rich youth and his stylish car conveys the tragedy of his family when all was lost in the moment of an accident. Yet the response of this Staatsburg family to their sorrow is not only comforting, but admirable: making the memory of their son the soul of an enchanted forest.

*Lewis Norrie Monument, 1930.* The Lewis Gordon Norrie Playground, a 17.3-acre parcel of land, was given to the citizens of Staatsburg by A. Gordon and Margaret L.M. Norrie in memory of their son, who died in an automobile accident while attending Princeton University. During the development of Mills-Norrie State Park, the playground was sold to New York State.

*The Railroad Station, 1905.* Before the advent of cars, the Staatsburg Railroad Station was busy with estate dwellers and their guests. The 1890 original station was demolished in 1913 to make room for two additional tracks. A new station was built, but was eventually demolished for lack of passengers.

*Firehouse, 1931.* The Staatsburg Fire Co. was first organized in 1894 with forty-one members. In 1909 the name was changed to the Dinsmore Hose Co., and by that time the company had eighty-three active members and thirteen honorary ones. The firehouse was completed in 1913, and the first motorized truck, a Sanford pumper, was purchased in 1926. The ambulance corps was established in 1968.

"*Old Homestead,*" *c. 1900.* Also known as Horan's Tavern, this building served as a small hotel for many years. It later became Cardinal Inn. It was located on the corner of the Old Post Road and River Road. From left to right are: Jim Horan, John Washington, Mrs. Horan, Mary Ellen Horan, Agnes, and Jimmy "Chappy" Horan.

*Stone's Boarding House.* Stone's Farm on the Albany Post Road was a summer hotel where city people came for fresh country air and good food. Entertainment consisted of rocking on the front porch while watching cars pass by, a good example of the Italian saying "Il dolce fare niente," meaning "The sweet doing nothing."

*The Old School.* Staatsburg, like Hyde Park, was always noted for having good quality schools. This photograph shows the old wooden building while the new one is being built. Outhouses were part of the scenery; separate ones are shown here, each being carefully screened. The playground was also divided for boys and girls. The old building was demolished in 1931.

*Staatsburg Union Free School.* When the new school was completed in 1931, Hyde Park students attended the high school here. The elementary grades were on the first floor, with grades seven to twelve on the second floor. Climbing the stairs meant that you had really grown up! Coming to school required busing—a new experience for most Hyde Park students. The building is part of Anderson School today.

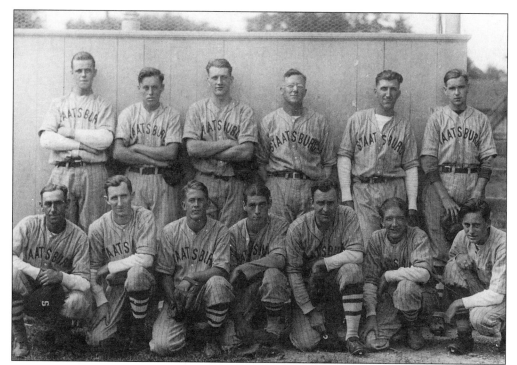

*Baseball Team, 1935.* Staatsburg always had a good baseball team and a ball lot that was well cared for by volunteers. The fellows in this 1935 team are, from left to right: (front row) Ed White, Joe Finnan, Lars Larson, Fran Kuhn, George Bodenstein, Gordon Plass, and Nelson Kidder; (back row) Howard Haug, Fred Kidder, Bud Hess, Ralph Simmons, Carlton Traver, and Lou Asher.

*Dinsmore Golf Course.* The families of wealth and leisure soon learned to enjoy this game, which originated in Scotland. With the donation of the land by Mr. Dinsmore, who was of Scottish descent, and the cooperation of other rich families, a 9-hole golf course was developed at the turn of the century, making it the second oldest privately owned golf course in the United States.

*CCC Camp Tents, 1935.* Civilian Conservation Corps Company 1274 was established at the Margaret Lewis Norrie State Park between 1934 and 1937. The men first lived in tents, while five forty-man barracks were constructed. A tool shed used by CCC has since been converted into a museum east of the environmental site.

*CCC Camp Barracks, 1935.* Between 1934 and 1942 approximately 4.5 million men served in the CCC, which was established by the Franklin D. Roosevelt administration. At Norrie State Park, the two-hundred-man company completed a system of roads, camping and picnic areas, a water system, and the Norrie Point Inn.

*Norrie Point Restaurant, 1936.* The Norrie Point Inn served the public as a restaurant from July 1, 1937, through the mid-1960s. Before this, Norrie Point was held in private ownership for many years. The Storm family was the last to reside there. Visitors reached the site, as they do today, either by auto or boat.

*Hendrick Hudson Day Liner.* The Day Liner Co. had several large river boats that made daily trips from New York to Albany and back. This trip was very pleasant and relaxing for those who cared to take it. The greatest pleasure, however, was for the boaters and swimmers who awaited to ride the swells of the river from the passing of the boats.

The

# VILLAGE OF STAATSBURG

# ROLL of HONOR

FRANKLIN ADRIANCE
ROBERT APPLETON
RAYMOND BANKS
RALPH BARTLEY
GEORGE BODENSTEIN
EDWARD BRANEN
REGINALD BRIGGS
JOSEPH BRUDER
WINFIELD BRUDER
ROBERT CHAPIN
GEORGE CLARK
GORDON COOKINGHAM
BERTHA CRAFT
HAROLD CRUSIUS
JOHN DAVISON
WILLIAM DONEGAN
EDWARD DOUGLASS
FRANK DOUGLASS
LAURENCE DOUGLASS
EDWARD FITZPATRICK
CHARLES FORMAN
PAUL GOLDFARB
WILLIAM GORMAN
LAWRENCE GRAHAM
STANLEY GRIFFEN
WILLIAM GRIFFEN
ALBERT HAGADORN
ALFONSO GELERMINO
JOHN ACKERMAN
JERRY TROWBRIDGE
ARVID BURKE

JAMES HAYES
EDWARD HENION
SHERIDAN HENION
JOHN HOBAN
FRANCIS HORAN
JAMES HORAN
KENNETH HORAN
ROBERT D. HUNTINGTON
HERBERT INGERSOLL
BRENTON JACKL
ALYDA KENDALL
CHARLES KENDALL
EDWARD KILLMER
KEARAN KIRBY
EDWARD KNAPP
RAYMOND KOLBENSKIE
FRANCIS KUHN
GERALD KUHN
JOHN KUHN
WALTER KUHN
CHRISTIAN LARSEN
BROSS LLOYD
HENRY MADSEN
JOSEPH MAHER
WILLIAM MAHER
HARRY MAIRKLE
WILLIAM McALLISTER
CLAUDE O'CALLAGHAN
ROBERT SMITH
ABRAM SMITH
JAMES FITZPATRICK

ROY MEHRINO
GEORGE MERRIHEW
ELNORA MERTE
HERMAN MERTE
EDWARD MURPHY
RICHARD OSTERHOUDT
JOHN SCHELLD
HENRY SCHMIDT
JAMES SCHULOFF
EDWARD SHERIDAN
JOHN SHERROD
★ JOSEPH SHERROD (K.S.)
RALPH SIMMONS, JR
WILLIAM SMITH
THOMAS STEENSON
HARRY STONE
RUSSELL STONE
KENNETH TABER
JAMES TODD
CARLTON TRAVER
GORDON TRUMBULL
JAMES VAIL
WARREN VAN KIRK
ROSS VAN WAGNER
VINCENT WALDRON
HARRY WISEMAN
RUSSELL WOODARD
ANDREW BRUDER
FRED KIDDER
ALFRED SMITH
GEORGE HESS

*Staatsburg Honor Roll.* Like all other villages and towns, Staatsburg sent its youth to the various services of our country in time of war. The people at home were proud of their boys and girls and placed their names on the honor roll at the corner of the Old Post Road and Market Street for all to see.